Student's Book
Stage 1

English in a quarter of the time!

The Callan ® Method was first developed and published
in 1960 by R.K. T. Callan.
This edition was published for the international market in 2012.

Copyright © R.K.T. Callan 2012

Student's Book – Stage 1
ISBN 978-1-908954-12-1

CALLAN and the CALLAN logo are registered trade marks
of Callan Works Limited, used under licence by Callan Publishing Limited

Printed in the EU

Conditions of sale

All rights reserved. No part of this publication may be reproduced, stored in a retrieval system or transmitted in any form or by any means, electronic, mechanical, photocopying, recording or otherwise, without the prior permission of the publishers.

This book is sold subject to the condition that it shall not by way of trade or otherwise be lent, re-sold, hired out or otherwise circulated without the publisher's prior consent in any form of binding or cover other than that in which it is published and without a similar condition including this condition being imposed on the subsequent purchaser.

Published by

CALLAN PUBLISHING LTD.
Orchard House, 45-47 Mill Way, Grantchester, Cambridge CB3 9ND
in association with CALLAN METHOD ORGANISATION LTD.

www.callan.co.uk

- Para obtener la traducción de este prefacio en español, visitar
  www.callan.co.uk/preface/es

- Per una traduzione di questa prefazione in Italiano, visitare il sito
  www.callan.co.uk/preface/it

- Para obter uma tradução deste prefácio em português, visite
  www.callan.co.uk/preface/pt

- Z polskim tłumaczeniem tego wstępu można zapoznać się na stronie
  www.callan.co.uk/preface/pl

- Pour obtenir la traduction de cette préface en français, rendez-vous sur le site
  www.callan.co.uk/preface/fr

- Bu önsözün Türkçe çevirisi için aşağıdaki web adresini ziyaret edin
  www.callan.co.uk/preface/tr

- 本序言的中文翻译，请访问
  www.callan.co.uk/preface/ch

- 前書きの日本語版の翻訳は次ページをご覧ください
  www.callan.co.uk/preface/jp

- للاطلاع على ترجمة هذه المقدمة باللغة العربية يرجى زيارة
  www.callan.co.uk/preface/ar

Welcome to the Callan Method

Learning English with the Callan™ Method is fast and effective!

The Callan Method is a teaching method created specifically to improve your English in an intensive atmosphere. The teacher is constantly asking questions, so you are hearing and using the language as much as possible. When you speak in the lesson, the teacher corrects your grammar and pronunciation mistakes, and you learn a lot from this correction.

The Callan Method teaches English vocabulary and grammar in a carefully programmed way, with systematic revision and reinforcement. In the lesson, there is a lot of speaking and listening practice, but there is also reading and writing so that you revise and consolidate what you have learned.

With the Callan Method, the teacher speaks quickly so that you learn to understand English when it is spoken at natural speed. This also means that everyone is concentrating hard all the time.

English in a quarter of the time

The Callan Method can teach English in a quarter of the time taken by any other method on the market. Instead of the usual 350 hours necessary to get the average student to the level of the Cambridge Preliminary English Test (PET), the Callan Method can take as little as 80 hours, and only 160 hours for the Cambridge First Certificate in English (FCE).

The method is suitable for students of all nationalities, and ages. It requires no equipment (not even a whiteboard) or other books, and can be used for classes at private schools, state schools and universities. It is also possible for students to use the books to practise with each other when they are not at school.

In addition to this, students can practise their English online using the interactive exercises, which are available to students who study at licensed schools. Ask your school for details.

The Callan Method in practice

A Callan Method English lesson is probably very different from lessons you have done in the past. You do not sit in silence, doing a reading comprehension test or a grammar exercise from a book. You do not have 'free conversation', where you only use the English you already feel comfortable with. Of course, activities like this can help you, but you can do them at home with a book, or in a coffee bar. In a Callan Method lesson, you are busy with important activities that you cannot do outside the classroom. You are listening to English all the time. You are speaking English a lot, and all your mistakes are corrected. You learn quickly because you are always surrounded by English. There is no silence and no time to get bored or lose your concentration. And it is also fun!

So, what exactly happens in a Callan Method lesson, and how does it work?

The teacher asks you questions

The Callan Method books are full of questions. Each question practises a word, an expression, or a piece of grammar. The teacher is standing, and asks the questions to the students one by one. You never know when the teacher will ask you, so you are always concentrating. When one student finishes answering one question, the teacher immediately starts to ask the next question.

The teacher speaks quickly

The teacher in a Callan Method lesson speaks quickly. This is because, in the real world, it is natural to speak quickly. If you want to understand normal English, you must practise listening to quick natural speech and become able to understand English without first translating into your language. This idea of not translating is at the centre of the Callan Method; this method helps you to start thinking in English.

Also, we do not want you to stop and think a lot about the grammar while you are speaking. We want you to speak as a reflex, instinctively. And do not worry about mistakes. You will, naturally, make a lot of mistakes in the lessons, but Callan Method teachers correct your mistakes, and you learn from the corrections. When you go home, of course it will help if you read your book, think about the grammar, study the vocabulary, and do all the things that language students do at home – but the lessons are times to practise your listening and speaking, with your books closed!

The teacher says every question twice, and helps you with the answer

In the lesson, the teacher speaks quickly, so we say the questions twice. This way, you have another chance to listen if you did not understand everything the first time.

The teacher then immediately says the beginning of the answer. This is to help you (and 'push' you) to start speaking immediately. So, for example:

Teacher: *"Are there two chairs in this room? Are there two chairs in this room? No, there aren't ..."*

Student (immediately): *"No, there aren't two chairs in this room; there are twelve chairs in this room."*

If the teacher does not 'push' you by giving you the beginning of the answer, you might start to think too much, and translate into your language.

The teacher will speak along with you all the time while you are saying your answer. So, if you forget a word or you are not sure what to say, you will always hear the next word or two from the teacher. You should repeat after the teacher, but immediately try again to continue with the answer yourself. You must always try to continue speaking, and only copy the teacher when you cannot continue alone. That way, you will become more confident and learn more quickly. Never simply wait for help from the teacher and then copy – you will not improve so quickly.

Long answers, with the same grammar as the question

We want you to practise your speaking as much as possible, so you always make complete sentences when you speak in the lesson, using the same grammatical structure as in the question. For example:

Teacher: *"About how many pages are there in this book?"*

Student: *"There are about two hundred pages in that book."*

In this way, you are not just answering a question; you are making full sentences with the vocabulary and the grammar that you need to learn.

Correction by imitation

With the Callan Method, the teacher corrects all your mistakes the moment you make them. The teacher corrects you by imitating (copying) your mistake and then saying the correct pronunciation/form of the word. For example, if you say "He come from Spain", the teacher quickly says "not come - **comes**". This correction by imitation helps you to hear the difference between your mistake and the proper English form. You should immediately repeat the correct word and continue with your sentence. You learn a lot from this correction of your mistakes, and constant correction results in fast progress.

Contracted forms

In the lesson, the teacher uses contractions (e.g. the teacher says "I don't" instead of "I do not"). This is because it is natural to use contractions in spoken English and you must learn to understand them. Also, if you want to sound natural when you speak, you must learn to use contractions.

Lesson structure

Every school is different, but a typical 50-minute Callan lesson will contain about 35 minutes of speaking, a 10-minute period for reading, and a 5-minute dictation. The reading practice and the dictation are often in the middle of the lesson.

In the reading part, you read and speak while the teacher helps you and corrects your mistakes. In the dictation, you practise your writing, but you are also listening to the teacher. So, a 50-minute Callan lesson is 50 minutes of spoken English with no silence!

No chatting

Although the Callan Method emphasises the importance of speaking practice, this does not mean chatting (free conversation). You learn English quickly with the Callan Method partly because the lessons are organised, efficient, fast and busy. There is no time wasted on chatting; this can be done before or after the lesson.

Chatting is not a good way to spend your time in an English lesson. First, only some of the students speak. Second, in a chat, people only use the English that they already know. Third, it is difficult for a teacher to correct mistakes during a conversation.

The Callan Method has none of these problems. All through the lesson, every student is listening and speaking, practising different vocabulary and structures, and learning from the correction of their mistakes. And nobody has time to get bored!

Repeat, repeat, repeat!

Systematic revision

In your native language, you sometimes read or hear a word that you do not already know. You usually need to read or hear this new word only once or twice in order to remember it and then use it yourself. However, when you are learning a foreign language, things are very different. You need to hear, see and use words and grammatical structures many times before you really know them properly. So your studies must involve a system of revision (repeating what you have studied before). This is absolutely essential. If there is no system of revision in your studies, you will forget what you have studied and will not be able to speak or understand better than before.

In every Callan Method lesson, of course you learn new English, practise it, and progress through your book. However, you also do a lot of revision so that you can really learn what you have studied. Your teacher can decide how much revision your class needs, but it will always be an important part of your studies.

Also, because there is a lot of revision, it is not important for you to understand everything the first time; it gets easier. The revision with Callan is automatic and systematic. Every day you do a lot of revision and then learn some new English.

Revision in reading and dictation too

The reading and dictation practice in the lessons is part of Callan's systematic revision as well. First, you learn a new word in the speaking part of the lesson; a few lessons later, you meet it again when you are reading; finally, the word appears in a dictation. This is all written into the Callan Method; it happens automatically.

Correcting your dictations

With the Callan Method, there is little or no homework to do, but it is very important that you correct your dictations. These are printed in your book and so you can easily correct them at home, on the bus, or wherever. It is important to do this because it helps you to learn the written forms of the words you have already studied in earlier lessons.

Your first lessons with the Callan Method

During your first lesson with the Callan Method, all of the questions and some of the vocabulary are new for you; you have not done any revision yet. For this reason, the teacher may not ask you many questions. You can sit and listen, and become more familiar with the method - the speed, the questions, the correction etc.

History of the Callan Method – Robin Callan

Robin Callan is the creator of the Callan Method. He owns the Callan School in London's Oxford Street. He also runs Callan Publishing Limited, which supplies Callan Method books to schools all over the world.

Robin Callan grew up in Ely, Cambridgeshire, England. In his early twenties, he went to Italy to teach English in Salerno. Although he enjoyed teaching, Robin thought that the way in which teachers were expected to teach their lessons was inefficient and boring. He became very interested in the mechanisms of language learning, and was sure that he could radically improve the way English was taught.

He remained in Italy and started to write his own books for teaching English. He used these in his own classes and, over the following ten years, gained an immense amount of practical experience and a reputation for teaching English quickly and effectively.

When he returned to England, he opened his school in Oxford Street. As the method became more and more popular with students, the school grew and moved to larger premises. Robin continued to write his Callan Method books, and today the method is used by schools all over the world.

Robin Callan has always been passionate about English literature, especially poetry. For this reason, he bought The Orchard Tea Garden in Grantchester, near Cambridge, which attracts thousands of tourists each year. Throughout the 20th century, it was a popular meeting place for many famous Cambridge University students and important figures from English literature, such as Rupert Brooke, Virginia Woolf and E.M. Forster. Today, it is also home to the Rupert Brooke Museum.

Mr Callan now lives in Grantchester, but still plays an active role in the management of the Callan School in London.

The Callan School in London's Oxford Street

The largest private school in London

The Callan School in Oxford Street is the largest private school in London teaching English as a foreign language. Depending on the time of year, the school employs between 60 and 100 teachers and has an average of 1600 students passing through its doors every day. This number rises to more than 2000 in the middle of summer, similar to a small university.

Websites

Please visit the following websites for more information:

Callan Method http://www.callan.co.uk

Lots of information, including a list of schools around the world that use the method

Callan School London http://www.callanschoollondon.com/en/callan-school

All you need to know about the largest private English language school in London

How Callan Method Stages compare to CEFR* levels and University of Cambridge General English exams

Common European Framework of Reference

It is difficult to compare the Callan Method books directly with the CEFR levels and Cambridge exams, but below is an approximate guide.

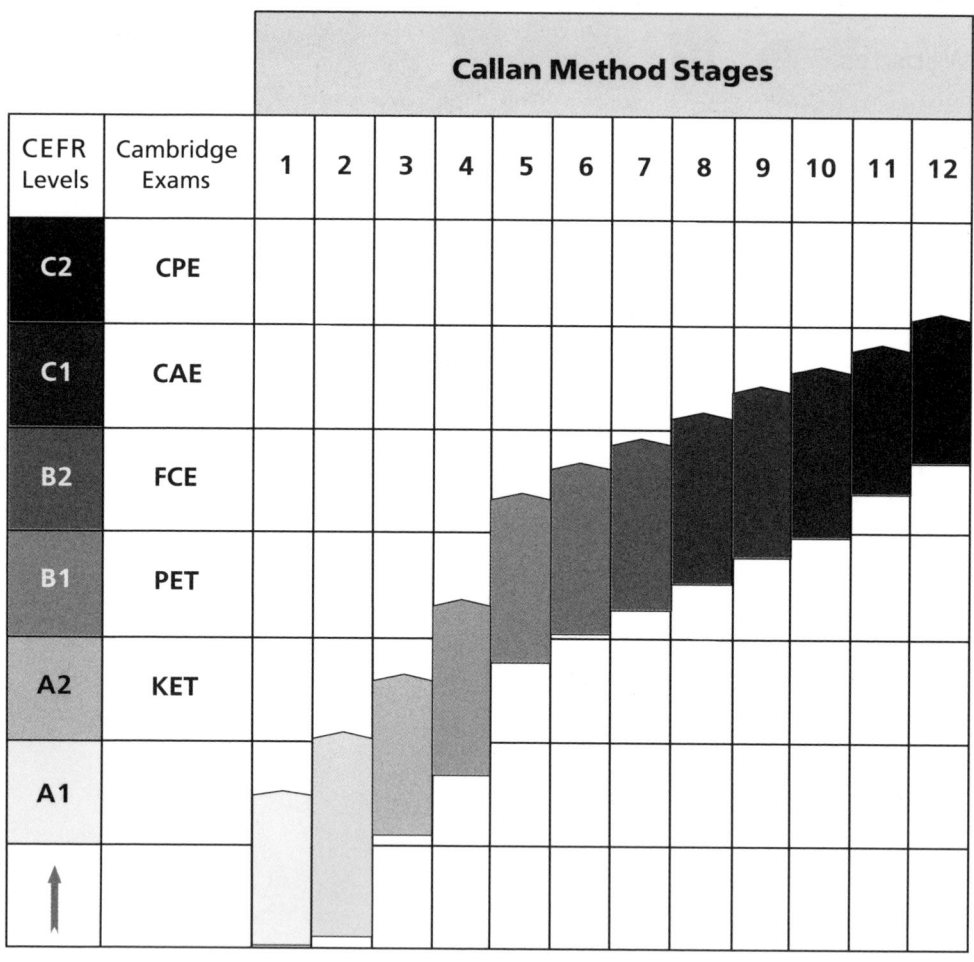

STAGE 1

LESSON 1

1 **pen   pencil   book   a**

   what is (what's)   this   it is (it's)

   What's this?   It's a pen

2   *See Chart 1* (at the end of this book)

   table   chair   light   wall

   floor   room   ceiling   window

   door   clock   box   picture

   is this?   yes

   Is this a pen?   Yes, it's a pen

   no, it is not (isn't)

   Is this a pen?   No, it isn't a pen; it's a pencil
   Is this a pencil?   No, it isn't a pencil; it's a book

3   *See Chart 1*

   long   short   the   contraction

   Is the pen short?   No, the pen isn't short; it's long
   Is the pencil long?   No, the pencil isn't long; it's short
   Is the room short?   No, the room isn't short; it's long

large	small
Is the table small?	No, the table isn't small; it's large
Is the box large?	No, the box isn't large; it's small

4
city	town	village

London is a city. Windsor is a town. Grantchester is a village.

Is (London) a village?	No, (London) isn't a village; it's a city
Is (Windsor) a city?	No, (Windsor) isn't a city; it's a town
Is (Grantchester) a town?	No, (Grantchester) isn't a town; it's a village

or

Is the table long or short?	The table's …
Is a city large or small?	A city's large

See Chart 1

man	woman	boy	girl

What's this?	It's a man. It's a woman. It's a boy. It's a girl.
Is this a girl?	No, it isn't a girl; it's a man
Is this a man?	No, it isn't a man; it's a woman
Is this a woman?	No, it isn't a woman; it's a boy
Is this a boy?	No, it isn't a boy; it's a girl

5

one	two	three	four	five
1	2	3	4	5

on	under	in

Is the pen in the book? — No, the pen isn't in the book; it's under the book

Is the pen under the book? — No, the pen isn't under the book; it's on the book

6  See Chart 1

Mr	Mrs	Jack	Anna

Is this Anna Brown? — No, it isn't Anna Brown; it's Mr Brown

Is this Mr Brown? — No, it isn't Mr Brown; it's Mrs Brown

Is this Mrs Brown? — No, it isn't Mrs Brown; it's Jack Brown

Is this Jack Brown? — No, it isn't Jack Brown; it's Anna Brown

 See Chart 1

black	white	green	brown

what colour?

7 What colour's this pencil? — This pencil's black, white etc.

six	seven	eight	nine	ten
6	7	8	9	10

where

Where's the pen? — The pen's on the book

Where's the book? — The book's on the table

Where's the pen? — The pen's under the table

Where's the picture? — The picture's on the wall

Where's the light? — The light's on the ceiling

LESSON 2

8  *See Chart 1*

I am	I'm
you are	you're
he is	he's
she is	she's
it is	it's

Am I ...?	Yes, you're ...
Are you ...?	Yes, I'm ...
Is he Mr Brown?	Yes, he's Mr Brown
Is she Mrs Brown?	Yes, she's Mrs Brown

9

I am not	I'm not
you are not	you aren't
he is not	he isn't
she is not	she isn't
it is not	it isn't

Am I Mrs Brown?	No, you aren't Mrs Brown; you're ...
Are you Mr Brown?	No, I'm not Mr Brown; I'm ...
Is he Mr Smith?	No, he isn't Mr Smith; he's Mr Brown
Is she Mr Brown?	No, she isn't Mr Brown; she's Mrs Brown

in front of behind me you

Where's the table? — The table's in front of me

10 Is the wall in front of you? — No, the wall isn't in front of me; it's behind me

Is the table behind me? — No, the table isn't behind you; it's in front of you

 *See Chart 1*

him her house

Where's the house? — The house is behind him

Where's the house? — The house is behind her

Are you behind her? — No, I'm not behind her; I'm in front of her

11 Am I in front of him? — No, you aren't in front of him; you're behind him

standing sitting

Are you standing on the floor? — No, I'm not standing on the floor; I'm sitting on the chair

Am I sitting on the chair? — No, you aren't sitting on the chair; you're standing on the floor

Are you standing in front of me? — No, I'm not standing in front of you; I'm sitting in front of you

taking from putting on

Am I putting the book on the floor? — No, you aren't putting the book on the floor; you're taking the book from the table

Am I taking the pen from the table? — No, you aren't taking the pen from the table; you're putting the book on the table

12

opening	**closing**
Am I closing the door?	No, you aren't closing the door; you're opening the book
Am I opening the window?	No, you aren't opening the window; you're closing the book

doing	**what am I doing?**
What am I doing?	You're taking the book from the table
What am I doing?	You're opening the book
What am I doing?	You're closing the book
What am I doing?	You're putting the book on the table

See Chart 1

which

13

Which pencil's black?	This pencil's black
Which pencil's white?	This pencil's white
Which pencil's green?	This pencil's green
Which pencil's brown?	This pencil's brown

open	**closed**
Which book's open?	This book's open
Which book's closed?	This book's closed

LESSON 3

14  *See Chart 1*

this	**that**	**chart**

What colour's this pencil? — This pencil's black
What colour's that pencil? — That pencil's white
Where's this pencil? — This pencil's on the Chart
Where's that pencil? — That pencil's on the wall

eleven	**twelve**	**thirteen**	**fourteen**	**fifteen**
11	12	13	14	15

plural	**of**	**etc.**

15 What's the plural of "book"? — The plural of "book" is "books"
What's the plural of "clock"? — The plural of "clock" is "clocks"
What's the plural of "wall"? — The plural of "wall" is "walls"

we are	**we're**

Are we sitting? — Yes, we're sitting
Where are we sitting? — We're sitting on the chairs

 *See Chart 1*

they are	they're
Are they standing?	Yes, they're standing
Where are they standing?	They're standing in front of the house

we are not	we aren't
Are we standing?	No, we aren't standing; we're sitting
Are we sitting on the floor?	No, we aren't sitting on the floor; we're sitting on the chairs

they are not	they aren't
Are they sitting?	No, they aren't sitting; they're standing
Are they standing behind the house?	No, they aren't standing behind the house; they're standing in front of the house

red	blue	yellow	grey

See Chart 1

What colour's this pencil?	This pencil's red, blue etc.

these	those	and

What colour's this pencil?	This pencil's black
What colour's that pencil?	That pencil's white
What colour are these pencils?	These pencils are black and green
What colour are those pencils?	Those pencils are white and brown
Where are these pencils?	These pencils are on the Chart

Where are those pencils?	Those pencils are on the wall
What colour are these chairs?	These chairs are ...
What colour are those chairs?	Those chairs are ...

men   **women**   **say**

What's the plural of "man"?	The plural of "man" is "men"
What's the plural of "woman"?	The plural of "woman" is "women"

sixteen	seventeen	eighteen	nineteen	twenty
16	17	18	19	20

 See Chart 1

clothes

What are these?	These are clothes

shoe	boot	sock	trousers	jacket
suit	shirt	tie	hat	bag

What's this?	It's a shoe, boot etc.
What are these?	These are trousers

 See Chart 2

alphabet   **letter**

What letter's this?	A, B, etc.

vowel	consonant

These are the five vowels: A, E, I, O, U.

What are these?	These are the five vowels
What are the five vowels?	The five vowels are A, E, I ,O, U

19 **The letters B, C, D etc. are consonants.**

Is the letter B a vowel?	No, the letter B isn't a vowel; it's a consonant

before	after
Which letter's before E?	D's before E
Which letter's after I?	J's after I
Which letter's before Z?	Y's before Z
Which letter's after G?	H's after G

LESSON 4

20 between

Which letter's between D and F?	E's between D and F
Which letter's between H and J?	I's between H and J
Which letter's between Q and S?	R's between Q and S

us

Where's the table?	The table's in front of us
Are the walls in front of us?	No, the walls aren't in front of us; they're behind us
Is the table behind us?	No, the table isn't behind us; it's in front of us

 *See Chart 1*

21 them

Where's the house?	The house's behind them
Are you behind them?	No, I'm not behind them; I'm in front of them
Am I in front of them?	No, you aren't in front of them; you're behind them

student   teacher

Am I a student?	No, you aren't a student; you're the teacher
Are you the teacher?	No, I'm not the teacher; I'm a student

 *See Chart 3*

thirty	forty	fifty	sixty	seventy	eighty
30	40	50	60	70	80

ninety	hundred	thousand	million	number
90	100	1,000	1,000,000	

22 What number's this?   30, 40 etc.

What numbers are these?   30–13; 40–14 etc.

What number's this?   313   1,815   1,950,630

plus   equals   2 + 2 = 4

What's this?   It's 2 + 2 = 4

how much

How much is 13 plus 5?   13 plus 5 equals 18

How much is   18 + 40   5 + 10
               60 + 19   6 + 3
               16 + 30   20 + 15
               90 + 15   10 + 30

23 there is   there's

Is there a pen on this book?   Yes, there's a pen on this book

Is there a light on the ceiling?   Yes, there's a light on the ceiling

Is there a bag in this room?   Yes, there's a bag in this room

there are	**now**
Is there a pen on the book?	Yes, there's a pen on the book
Are there two pens on the book now?	Yes, there are two pens on the book now
Are there (12) chairs in this room?	Yes, there are (12) chairs in this room
Are there (2) pictures on these walls?	Yes, there are (2) pictures on these walls

there is not	**there isn't**
Is there a pen on the book?	No, there isn't a pen on the book
Is there a book on the floor?	No, there isn't a book on the floor
Is there a clock on the table?	No, there isn't a clock on the table

there are not	**there aren't**
Are there three clocks on that wall?	No, there aren't three clocks on that wall; there's one clock on that wall
Are there a hundred pictures in this room?	No, there aren't a hundred pictures in this room; there are ... pictures in this room
Are there a thousand chairs in this room?	No, there aren't a thousand chairs in this room; there are ... chairs in this room

high	**low**	**but**
Is the chair high?		No, the chair isn't high; it's low
Is the wall low?		No, the wall isn't low; it's high
Is the table high?		No, the table isn't high; it's low

LESSON 5

25 | imperative | take! | put! | open! |

| close! | please |

The imperative is "take!", "put!", "open!", "close!" etc.

What's he/she doing? He's/She's taking the book

Open the book, please.

What's he/she doing? He's/She's opening the book

Close the book, please.

What's he/she doing? He's/She's closing the book

Put the book on the table, please.

What's he/she doing? He's/She's putting the book on the table

26 *See Chart 1*

| here | there |

Where's the black pencil? The black pencil's here in front of me

Where's the white pencil? The white pencil's there on the wall

Are you sitting there? No, I'm not sitting there; I'm sitting here

Is the white pencil here in front of you? No, the white pencil isn't here in front of me; it's there on the Chart

capital	England	Russia	Greece	China
London	Moscow		Athens	Beijing

What's the capital of England? — London's the capital of England

What's the capital of Russia? — Moscow's the capital of Russia

27 What's the capital of Greece? — Athens's the capital of Greece

What's the capital of China? — Beijing's the capital of China

reading	writing

What am I doing? — You're reading the book *hciendo*

What am I doing? — You're writing in the book *describiendo*

Am I writing in the book? — No, you aren't writing in the book; you're reading the book

Am I reading the book? — No, you aren't reading the book; you're writing in the book *riding*

 See Chart 1

coat	tights	dress	skirt	scarf
blouse	pullover		pocket	handkerchief

What's this? — It's a coat, dress etc.

What are these? — These are tights

28 **how many?**

How many pictures are there on these walls? — There are ... pictures on these walls

How many clocks are there in this room? — There's one clock in this room

How many chairs are there in this room?	There are ... chairs in this room
How many teachers are there in this room?	There's one teacher in this room

going to

What am I doing?	You're going to the door
What am I doing?	You're going to the window
Where am I going?	You're going to the wall
Am I going to the door?	No, you aren't going to the door; you're going to the window

(handwritten note near "aren't": "are not")

LESSON 6

29 | **Europe** | **Asia** | **Italy** | **France** | **India** |

Is Greece in Asia? No, Greece isn't in Asia; it's in Europe

Is India in Europe? No, India isn't in Europe; it's in Asia

Are France and Italy in Asia? No, France and Italy aren't in Asia; they're in Europe

See Chart 2

first	**second**	**third**	**fourth**
1st	2nd	3rd	4th
fifth	**sixth**	**twelfth**	**twentieth**
5th	6th	12th	20th
cardinal		**ordinal**	

30 What are the cardinal numbers? The cardinal numbers are 1, 2, 3, etc.

What are the ordinal numbers? The ordinal numbers are 1st, 2nd, 3rd, etc.

Which is the first letter of the alphabet? A's the first letter of the alphabet

Which is the third letter of the alphabet? C's the third letter of the alphabet

Which is the fifth letter of the alphabet? E's the fifth letter of the alphabet

Which is the twelfth letter of the alphabet? L's the twelfth letter of the alphabet

Which is the thirteenth letter of the alphabet? M's the thirteenth letter of the alphabet

Which is the twentieth letter of the alphabet?	T's the twentieth letter of the alphabet
Which is the twenty-first letter?	U's the twenty-first letter
Which is the twenty-third letter?	W's the twenty-third letter
Which is the twenty-fifth letter?	Y's the twenty-fifth letter

31 last

Which's the last letter of the alphabet?	Z's the last letter of the alphabet
Is A the last letter of the alphabet?	No, A isn't the last letter of the alphabet; it's the first letter of the alphabet

give

Take the book, please.	
Give me the book, please.	
What's he/she doing?	He's/She's giving you the book
Take the book, please.	
Give him/her the book, please.	
What's he/she doing?	He's/She's giving him/her the book

32 French   German   Italian   English

Are you (French) or (German)?	No, I'm not (French) or (German); I'm ...
Am I (Italian) or (French)?	No, you aren't (Italian) or (French); you're (English)
Are the students (German) or (English)?	The students are ...

my	**your**
Is this your book?	No, it isn't my book; it's your book
Is that my dress?	No, it isn't your dress; it's my dress

 See Chart 1

his	**her**
Are these his boots?	No, they aren't his boots; they're her boots
Are these her shoes?	No, they aren't her shoes; they're his shoes
Is this his bag?	No, it isn't his bag; it's her bag
Is this her suit?	No, it isn't her suit; it's his suit
What colour's his suit?	His suit's black

our	**your**	**their**
Are these our shoes?		No, they aren't our shoes; they're their shoes
What colour are their shoes?		Their shoes are black
Are these their books?		No, these aren't their books; they're our books
Where are our books?		Our books are on the table(s)

all

Are all the walls in this room white (or green or blue etc.)?	Yes, all the walls in this room are white
Are all the books in this room English books?	Yes, all the books in this room are English books
Are all the students sitting?	Yes, all the students are sitting

LESSON 7

35 **person**   **people**

What's the plural of "person"?   The plural of "person" is "people"

How many people are there in this room?   There are ... people in this room

How many people are there in this town?   There are ... people in this town

coming from

What am I doing?   You're coming from the door

Am I coming from the window?   No, you aren't coming from the window; you're going to the window

36 Am I going to the window?   No, you aren't going to the window; you're coming from the window

touch

What am I doing?   You're touching the wall

What am I doing?   You're touching the picture

Touch your tie (or dress, shoe etc.), please.

What's he/she doing?   He's/She's touching his/her ...

See Chart 2

sentence

What's this?   It's a sentence

word	verb	use	for	action

(handwritten: o palabras)

What's this?	It's a word
37 How many words are there in this sentence?	There are seven words in this sentence
Which's the first word of this sentence?	"Verbs" is the first word of this sentence
Which's the third word of this sentence?	"Words" is the third word of this sentence
Which's the fifth word of this sentence?	"Use" is the fifth word of this sentence
Which's the sixth word?	"For" is the sixth word of this sentence
Which's the last word?	"Actions" is the last word of this sentence

(handwritten above "sentence": phrases; handwritten below "first": cual)

question mark	?	full stop	.
comma	,	colon	:
semi-colon	;		

What's this?	It's a question mark
What's this?	It's a full stop
What's this?	It's a comma
What's this?	It's a colon
What's this?	It's a semi-colon

38 **umbrella**

What word's this?	It's the word "umbrella"
Is there an umbrella on the table?	No, there isn't an umbrella on the table

pronounce

Pronounce this word, please.	What
What's he/she doing?	He's/She's pronouncing the word "what"
Pronounce this word, please.	Colour
What's he/she doing?	He's/She's pronouncing the word "colour"

a   an   the /ðə/   the /ði:/

We say a book, but an umbrella. The book, but the umbrella. Before a consonant we say "a" – a book. Before a vowel we say "an" – an umbrella. Before a consonant we say "the" – the book. Before a vowel we say "the" – the umbrella.

39 Pronounce these words, please.   a book – an umbrella; the book – the umbrella

body

What's this?	This is the body
Is this her body?	No, it isn't her body; it's your body

part   foot   feet

What part of the body is this?	This part of the body is the foot
What's the plural of "foot"?	The plural of "foot" is "feet"

leg   **back**   **arm**   **wrist**

hand   **finger**   **thumb**

What's this?   It's a leg, <u>the</u> back, <u>an</u> arm, a wrist etc.

right	**wrong**
2 + 2 = 7: is that right?	No, it isn't right; it's wrong
The wall's high: is that wrong?	No, it isn't wrong; it's right
Is it right you're Mr Brown?	No, it isn't right I'm Mr Brown; it's wrong. I'm ...

LESSON 8

41  See Chart 2

question	answer
What's this?	It's a question
What's this?	It's an answer
Is this an answer?	No, it isn't an answer; it's a question

meaning	
What's the meaning of the word "use" in ...?	The meaning of the word "use" in ... is "..."
What's the meaning of the word "table" in ...?	The meaning of the word "table" in ... is "..."
What's the meaning of the word "for" in ...?	The meaning of the word "for" in ... is "..."
What's the meaning of the word "chair" in ...?	The meaning of the word "chair" in ... is "..."
What's the meaning of the word "action" in ...?	The meaning of the word "action" in ... is "..."

42 **name**

What's my name?	Your name's ...
What's your name?	My name's ...

See Chart 1

What's his name?	His name's Mr Brown
What's her name?	Her name's Mrs Brown

| head | face | chin | mouth |
| nose | eye | ear | hair | tongue |

What's this? — It's the head etc.

43 remaining ~quedar, permanecer

What am I doing? — You're going to the window

What am I doing? — You're coming from the window

Are you going to the window? — No, I'm not going to the window; I'm remaining on the chair

Am I remaining on the chair? — No, you aren't remaining on the chair; you're going to the window

| country | Spain |

What's the name of your country? — ... is the name of my country

entre

What's the name of the country between England and Spain? — France's the name of the country between England and Spain

| translate | into |

44  See Chart 2

"Verbs are words we use for actions".

What am I doing? — You're translating a sentence from English into ...

Translate this sentence, please: "I am a student".

What's he/she doing? — He's/She's translating a sentence from English into ...

Translate this sentence, please: "The wall's high".

What's he/she doing? He's/She's translating a sentence from English into ...

Translate this sentence, please: "There are ten chairs in this room".

What's he/she doing? He's/She's translating a sentence from English into ...

who

Who am I? You're Mr Smith

Who are you? I'm Mr Rossi

Who's he? He's Jack Brown

45 Who's she? She's Anna Brown

Who are they? They're Mr and Mrs Brown

thing

How many things are there on this book? There are three things on that book

What's the name of this thing? The name of that thing is a tie

What colour's this thing? This thing's red

 See Chart 1

tall   short   Scandinavia

Is Mr Brown short? No, Mr Brown isn't short; he's tall

Is Anna Brown tall? No, Anna Brown isn't tall; she's short

Are the people of Scandinavia short? No, the people of Scandinavia aren't short; they're tall

46 **difference** whereas that

What's the difference between "tall" and "short" and "high" and "low"?
The difference between "tall" and "short" and "high" and "low" is that we use "tall" and "short" for people, whereas we use "high" and "low" for things

47 *Dictation 1*

What's this?/ It's a pen./ Is this/ a pencil/ or a book?/ Is the/ long table/ black?/ No, it isn't;/ it's white./ The short box/ is green./ A city is large/ but a village/ is small./ Is Mr Brown/ a man?/ Yes, he is./ Is Anna Brown/ a boy or a girl?/ She's a girl./ One, two, three,/ four, five./ Is the clock/ on the table/ or under the chair?/ No,/ it's on the wall./ What colour/ is the ceiling?

LESSON 9

48 | **asking** | **answering** |
|---|---|
| What's this? | It's a pen |
| What am I doing? | You're asking him/her a question |
| What's this? | It's a hand |
| Am I asking him/her a question? | Yes, you're asking him/her a question |
| What's this? | It's a head |
| What's he/she doing? | He's/She's answering your question |
| What's this? | It's a mouth |
| Is he/she answering my question? | Yes, he's/she's answering your question |
| Ask him/her a question, please. | |

49 **To have**

I have	I've
you have	you've
he has	he's
she has	she's
it has	it's
we have	we've
you have	you've
they have	they've

What's the meaning of the verb "to have"? The meaning of the verb "to have" is ...

What's the contraction of "I have, you have" etc.?	I've, you've etc.

50 | **got** | **with** | **generally** |
|---|---|---|

With the verb "have", we generally use the word "got" and we say "I've got", "you've got", "he's got" etc. We say "I have a pen" or "I have got a pen".

Have I got two eyes?	Yes, you've got two eyes
Have you got two ears?	Yes, I've got two ears
Has he got two legs?	Yes, he's got two legs
Has she got two hands?	Yes, she's got two hands
Have we got two heads?	Yes, we've got two heads
Have they got four arms?	Yes, they've got four arms

 *See Chart 4*

any? non-specific	yes, **some** no, **not any**
how many? specific	seven thirteen etc. **none**

51 | **specific** **positive** | **non-specific** **for example** | **negative** **important** |
|---|---|---|
| **when** | | |

The meaning of "any" and "some" is "...", but we use "any" in questions and negative sentences, and "some" in positive sentences. For example, we say "Are there any books on the table?" – "Yes, there are some books on the table", and we say "Are there any books on the floor?" – "No, there aren't any books on the floor".

We use "any" in a non-specific question, when the number is not important. For example, "Are there any books on the table?" – "Yes, there are some books on the table", or "No, there aren't any books on the table". If the number is important, we use "How many" and there is a specific answer – "one", "two", "three" etc., or "none".

What is the meaning of the words "any" and "some"?
                              The meaning of the words "any" and "some" is ...

What's the difference between "any" and "some"?
                              The difference between "any" and "some" is that we use "any" in questions and negative sentences, whereas we use "some" in positive sentences

any

Are there any books on this table?   Yes, there are some books on this table

Are there any pictures on these walls?   Yes, there are some pictures on these walls

Have you got any shoes on your feet?   Yes, I've got some shoes on my feet

not any

Are there any books on the floor?   No, there aren't any books on the floor

Are there any pictures on that chair?   No, there aren't any pictures on that chair

Are there any chairs on the table?   No, there aren't any chairs on the table

none	class	classroom

How many books are there on the table?   There are ... books on the table

How many books are there on the floor?   There are none

How many pictures are there on these walls?   There are ... pictures on these walls

How many pictures are there on that chair?   There are none

How many students are there in this classroom?   There are ... students in this classroom

How many students are there sitting on the floor?   There are none

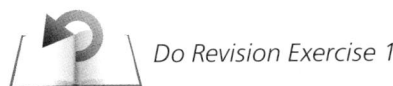 *Do Revision Exercise 1*

Revision exercises

In your book, you sometimes see 'Do Revision Exercise ...'. These exercises are at the end of each stage, and you can do them at home. This is a good idea because these exercises give you extra practice with the English you are learning at school. With the Callan Method, you learn quickly, but if you want to learn more quickly, you should study with your book, listen to the audio files, and do the revision exercises.

Write long answers to all the questions, like the answers that you say in the lessons. Then correct the exercise by looking at the printed answers in your book. Remember, the exercises are not for class; you do them outside the lesson for extra practice.

Revision Exercise 1 (Lessons 1 – 5)

1. Is London a village?
2. Is a city large or small?
3. Are you standing on the floor?
4. What's the plural of "book"?
5. What's the plural of "man"?
6. What's the plural of "woman"?
7. What are the five vowels?
8. Is the letter "B" a vowel?
9. Which letter's before "E"?
10. Which letter's after "G"?
11. Which letter's between "H" and "J"?
12. Are you the teacher?
13. How much is 13 plus 5?
14. Is there a light on the ceiling?
15. Is there a clock on the table?
16. Are there a hundred pictures in this room?
17. Is the wall low?
18. What's the capital of England?
19. What's the capital of Greece?
20. How many clocks are there in this room?

Answers

1. No, London isn't a village; it's a city.
2. A city's large.
3. No, I'm not standing on the floor; I'm sitting on the chair.
4. The plural of "book" is "books".
5. The plural of "man" is "men".
6. The plural of "woman" is "women".

7   The five vowels are "A E I O U".
8   No, the letter "B" isn't a vowel; it's a consonant.
9   D's before E.
10 H's after G.
11 I's between H and J.
12 No, I'm not the teacher; I'm a student.
13 13 plus 5 equals 18.
14 Yes, there's a light on the ceiling.
15 No, there isn't a clock on the table.
16 No, there aren't a hundred pictures in this room; there are ... pictures in this room.
17 No, the wall isn't low; it's high.
18 London's the capital of England.
19 Athens's the capital of Greece.
20 There's one clock in this room.

Demonstration Charts

Chart 1

Chart 2

1	2	3	4	5	6	7
Aa	Bb	Cc	Dd	Ee	Ff	Gg

14	15	16	17	18	19	20
Nn	Oo	Pp	Qq	Rr	Ss	Tt

a e i o u

Verbs are words

What colour is the book?

a book

the book

Chart 2

8	9	10	11	12	13
Hh	Ii	Jj	Kk	Ll	Mm

21	22	23	24	25	26
Uu	Vv	Ww	Xx	Yy	Zz

?   .   ,   :   ;

(handwritten annotations: question, full stop, comma, colon, way, semi-colon)

we use for actions.

The book is blue

an umbrella
the umbrella

Chart 3

13	30
14	40
15	50
16	60
17	70
18	80
19	90
20	100
	1,000
	1,000,000

313

1,815

1,950,630

2 + 2 = 4

1 × 5 = 5

2 × 5 = 10

3 × 5 = 15

4 × 5 = 20

```
  13
+ 30
────
  43
```

```
  15
+ 50
────
  65
```

Chart 4

| non-specific | **Any?** |
| specific | **How many?** |

| non-specific | **Anybody?** |
| specific | **Who?** |

| non-specific | **Anything?** |
| specific | **What?** |

Yes, some
No, not any

Seven etc.
None

Yes, somebody
No, not anybody

Mrs Brown etc.
Nobody

Yes, something
No, not anything

A light etc.
Nothing

Index

a 1, 38	consonant 18	hat 18	my 32
action 36	contraction 3	he has / he's 49	name 42
after 19	country 43	he is / he's 8	negative 50
all 34	difference 46	he is not / he isn't 9	nine 7
alphabet 18	doing 12	head 42	nineteen 17
an 38	door 2	her 10	ninety 21
and 16	dress 27	her 32	no, it is not (isn't) 2
answer 41	ear 42	here 26	non-specific 50
answering 48	eight 7	high 24	none 52
any 51	eighteen 17	him 10	nose 42
arm 39	eighty 21	his 32	not any 52
Asia 29	eleven 14	house 10	now 23
asking 48	England 26	how many? 28	number 21
Athens 26	English 32	how much 22	of 14
back 39	equals 22	hundred 21	on 5
bag 18	etc. 14	I am / I'm 8	one 5
before 19	Europe 29	I am not / I'm not 9	open 13
behind 9	eye 42	I have / I've 49	open! 25
Beijing 26	face 42	imperative 25	opening 12
between 20	feet 39	important 51	or 4
black 6	fifteen 14	in 5	ordinal 29
blouse 27	fifth 5th 29	in front of 9	our 33
blue 16	fifty 21	India 29	part 39
body 39	finger 39	into 43	pen 1
book 1	first 1st. 29	is this? 2	pencil 1
boot 18	five 5	it has / it's 49	people 35
box 2	floor 2	it is (it's) 1	person 35
boy 4	foot 39	it is / it's 8	picture 2
brown 6	for 36	it is not / it isn't 9	please 25
but 24	for example 51	Italian 32	plural 14
capital 26	forty 21	Italy 29	plus 22
cardinal 29	four 5	jacket 18	pocket 27
ceiling 2	fourteen 14	large 3	positive 51
chair 2	fourth 4th 29	last 31	pronounce 38
chart 14	France 29	leg 39	pullover 27
chin 42	French 32	letter 18	put! 25
China 26	full stop 37	light 2	putting on 11
city 4	generally 50	London 26	question 41
class 52	German 32	long 3	question mark ? ... 37
classroom 52	girl 4	low 24	reading 27
clock 2	give 31	man 4	red 16
close ! 25	going to 28	me 9	remaining 43
closed 13	got 50	meaning 41	right 40
closing 12	Greece 26	men 17	room 2
clothes 17	green 6	million 21	Russia 26
coat 27	grey 16	Moscow 26	say 17
colon : 37	hair 42	mouth 42	Scandinavia 45
coming from 35	hand 39	Mr 6	scarf 27
comma , ... 37	handkerchief 27	Mrs 6	second 2nd 29

semi-colon ; 37	thing 45	yes 2
sentence 36	third 3rd. 29	you 9
seven 7	thirteen 14	you are / you're 8
seventeen 17	thirty 21	you are not /
seventy 21	this 1	you aren't 9
she has / she's 49	this 14	you have / you've ... 49
she is / she's 8	those 16	you have / you've ... 49
she is not / she isn't .. 9	thousand 21	your 33
shirt 18	three 5	your 32
shoe 18	thumb 39	
short 3	tie 18	
short 45	tights 27	
sitting 11	to have 49	
six 7	tongue 42	
sixteen 17	touch 36	
sixth 6th 29	town 4	
sixty 21	translate 43	
skirt 27	trousers 18	
small 3	twelfth 12th 29	
sock 18	twelve 14	
some 50	twentieth 20th 29	
Spain 43	twenty 17	
specific 50	two 5	
standing 11	umbrella 38	
student 21	under 5	
suit 18	us 20	
table 2	use 36	
take! 25	verb 36	
taking from 11	village 4	
tall 45	vowel 18	
teacher 21	wall 2	
ten 7	we are / we're 15	
that 14	we are not /	
that 46	we aren't 15	
the 3	we have / we've 49	
the 38	what am I doing? ... 12	
the 38	what colour? 6	
their 33	what is (what's) 1	
them 21	when 51	
there 26	where 7	
there are 23	whereas 46	
there are not /	which 12	
there aren't 24	white 6	
there is / there's 23	who 44	
there is not /	window 2	
there isn't 24	with 50	
these 16	woman 4	
they are not /	women 17	
they aren't 16	word 36	
they are /	wrist 39	
they're 15	writing 27	
they have /	wrong 40	
they've 49	yellow 16	

Notes

Coat → abrigo
tights →
dress → vestido
pullover →
handkerchief →
blouse → clinex
read/ing → leer/leiendo
what am I doing? → que estoy haciendo

- there is → there is 1 teacher in this room
  ↓ → hay
  singular

- there are → there are 14 cheers in this room
  ↓ → hay
  plural

When → cuando
why → porque
white board → pizarra
his → su
large → grande

| I wake up at 8 am | ← How many word are there in this sentence? they are 6 words in this sentence
                                       what is the first word of this sentence?
                                       I is the first word of this sentence

6 words ↓   ↓
        verb preposition

1 2 3 4 5 6 sentence

Words → palabras (weurd pronunciation)
; → semi colon
? → question
: → colon
. → full stop
, → comma

wrong → incorrecto
right → correcto
meaning → significado
of → de
think/ing → pensar/ando

Notes

What is his/her name? | what → que, cual
her name is Carrie
└ es para mujeres

his name is Moha
└ para hombre

what is your haven't? I'm not haven't enesind
remaining: quedarse, permanecer
Are you going to the window? I'm not going to the window
I remaining on the chair

who is it?   who is coming to dinner tonigh? (breakfast/lunch)
└ ¿quien es
                quien viene a cenar esta noche
respuesta: my friend fernondo is coming to dinner tonight

who is he coming with?
    con quien viene
he's coming with his girlfriend
    él vendra con su novia

are you busy tomorrow? I'm not busy tomorrow
      (↓ visit
       ↓ ocupado)

unemployed → desempleado

We use "tall" and "short" for the people
nosotros usamos tall y short para los persone
whereas we use "high" and "low" for "things"
mientras nosotros usamos corto y largo para los cosas
think → pensar
forward →

backward
to think forward →
feel → sentir   feeling → sintiendo

Notes

can't → poder   I can't clean here → puedes limpiar aqui
I can't → yo puedo
nobody can't think for you? nadie piensa por ti

I cannot think for you?
→ yo no puedo pensar en ti
pain → dolor, enfermedad
happiness → felicidad
feelings →
any → alguna, algunos, cualquier/a | not any → ninguno/a
                  hay
are there any books on the floor? no, they aren't any books on the floor.

do you agree with me?
             A
tu estas deacuerdo conmigo

ask → una pregunta
about → sobre (I'm ringing to ask for some information about opening a new account.

tell → contar, decir, platicar

putting on → dejando en

taking from → cosiendo de

walk → andar
work → trabaja

where is the table? is front of us
                         → estado   esta delante nuestro
what have you been up to today? it's good to be busy...
                                             → mantenerse
... isn't it (innit) / it's good to keep one self busy

what have you been up today?
 I been to running today / I went to my brother's house

Scarf → bufanda
I want buy to second book

Notes

is it raining now? no it isn't raining now
is it windy today it isn't windy today
   ↳ viento

[present continious] → is it snowing now? no it isn't snowing now

[future tense] → will it rain tomorrow? I am not really sure if it'll rain tomorrow, because I haven't looked at the whether forecast.
    lo tiempo   prevision/pronostico

                  no gusta
do you [dislike (don't like)] the cinema? I don't dislike the cinema, I like the the cinema

                  su   desk
what's he doing?
he's puting his left hand on that book
She's puting her right hand on that book

puedes escribir water en la pizarra?
Significado de are solo?   ejemplo: all the students are sitting?
                            yes all the students are sitting

present simple   past simple

I like the cinema ⟷ I liked the cinema
I go to the station ⟷ I went to the station
I eat chicken and potatoes ⟷ I ate chicken and potatoes
I live in england ⟷ I lived in England
I don't care (no me importa) ⟷ I didn't care

them → ellos

Biggest →   laugh → reírse
   neither → ni uno ni otro

Notes

How's the weather today? It's raining today (it's wet)
How's the temperature? the temperature is 11° degree
              → caliente
it's very warm today, isn't it? no it's not very warm today,
                                 (it's n't)
it's very cold today.

do you prefer the warm weather, or the cold weather? I prefer the warm weather.

Is New Delhi a village or a town? No, New Delhi is neither a village, nor a town, It's a city.

llevo viviendo 2 meses →

                                            (8:30)
What time do you leave home? I leave home at half past eight
                    → preguntando   una
What I am doing? You'r asking her a question
                    → respondiendo ella → present
what's she doing? she's answering your question.

                → orejas
have I got two ears? Yes you've got two ears

Notes